"A. D. D." or "Not to Be"

Linda J. Anderson

Linda J. Anderson

Tulsa, Oklahoma

A.D.D. OR NOT TO BE

Published by Insight Publishing Group
8801 S. Yale, Suite 410
Tulsa, OK 74137
918-493-1718

ISBN 1-932503-42-0
Library of Congress catalog card number: 2004113891

Printed in the United States of America

Dedication

To my wonderful, loving and supportive husband, Russell, and my four awesome children; Tyler, Michael, Darlene, and April. I love you all very much. You truly have enriched my life. None of this would have been possible without you all. You are the best!

Contents

Foreword

I met Linda in 1999 while I was serving as acting Assistant Principal of their school. She told me about their family. Like many other parents she raved about her children. It was wonderful to have a parent actively involved in their children's education. She relayed to me her family's story of strife and struggle. The Andersons had adopted four African-American children with a horrific story. The kids had attendance problems, academic deficiencies, and behavior issues. This is the typical description of inner-city African-American foster children that usually fall by the nature of the education system and then drop out of school. But for Russ and Linda this was not an option. With a strong Christian foundation their story of revival began. Through tears, shouts, laughter, and pain, the Anderson children were destined for greatness. By changing the horrors and negative routines the children had embedded, all four children have realized success. Love, structure and discipline were key factors in their success.

It was this common thread that bonded me to the Andersons. I could truly see that Linda had a passion about not only educating her children, but others as well! As an educator I have often struggled with why students fall. Some educators believe it is culturally based, others feel it is social-economic factors, and still others feel that it is parental involvement. Although all three have merit and justification, I believe that parental involvement is the greatest contributing factor. Linda feels the same way. That is why she is so committed to being an active part of her children's education.

For Linda and Russ it has been a trying experience, but the rewards are almost unbelievable. Their story is true and noteworthy. The lessons contained in this book are life's lessons about child rearing. Remember everyone saying that there are no books or rules about raising children? I feel that the Anderson story can become a strong foundation to many struggling families that want what all parents want for their children—The Best!

Scott TenEyck
Principal and Friend
Toledo Public Schools

Acknowledgment

I want to thank a great person who has been a true and loyal friend—Janet DeVriendt. She gave many long hours to help type, edit, and proofread this book because she truly believes in its every word. As a teacher and friend, she has the same vision as myself—to help families who are searching for answers to their children's poor behavior patterns, requiring the use of medication. Thank you, Janet. I truly appreciate all that you have done.

Introduction

This book is the result of an eye-opener that I had after the adoption of our four children. I believe that many families will be able to identify with our problems and our searching for answers as well. This book is being written with the intent to help those who are ready to receive the answers they are looking for because they are willing to make the necessary changes to get the results that they are so desperately searching for.

After adopting our four children, who were ages 4, 5, 6, and 7 at the time, we noticed that they had many issues and behavior problems. They were doing poorly in school. They had a low level of concentration and a short attention span. They also had various behavior issues and all of these factors resulted in them being diagnosed with A.D.D. and A.D.H.D., requiring the use of medication. This greatly disturbed us.

So I began reading the accounts of their histories, which had been provided for us at the time of the adoption. I also began to do much research. One common factor that I noticed was related to their diet, or lack thereof. It was stated how they were undernourished, due to being abandoned and neglected many times. They had been eating high amounts of junk food—sugar, or whatever scrap they could find to keep from being hungry. In doing my research, I found that your body reacts to not being fed properly, and in turn affects how you function. If you are not getting the proper nutrients, you cannot concentrate, you cannot pay attention, you cannot sit still or function at a normal pace because your body is telling you that it is hungry. This alarmed me. All of the symptoms, all of the things that we were seeing—all of the areas of concentration, attention, and fidgeting—all were the result of poor nutrition. With the environment that they came from, the exposure to drugs and alcohol at an early age, and the lack of a proper diet, I concluded that all of these factors had contributed to the way that they were behaving. So therefore we began a change in their lifestyle.

In the following chapters I will be sharing with you what took place and the results that were achieved. You will truly be amazed. My children are now **all** *Honor Roll students. They are so healthy that they have had perfect attendance at school for the last three years. And best of all they are totally medication free and have been for the last five years.* People, what I am sharing with you works! *And I believe that if you are willing to invest the time that it takes to make the changes—that means the changing of your lifestyle, changing what you eat, changing what you speak—you can see the same results. I speak from personal experience.* It works! *Let's not wait a moment longer. Let's get started now!*

Chapter 1

How to Get Started

The question is, "How do I get started?" You must become a willing participant. Circumstances will not change left undone. You must be willing to change your lifestyle. It is very important that we understand that the reason we are unhappy or even just "fed up" today concerning ourselves and our life in general is a direct result of something we have done or that we are currently doing. So to make a change—to see our circumstances change for our children, for ourselves, and our lives—*We must change our lifestyle!*

Several things must be recognized in order to get started: Number 1 and the most important is time. Ask yourself:

- How much time am I willing to invest?
- How badly do I want to see my children change?
- How badly do I want to see my life changed?
- How badly do I want to see a change in my children's behavior?

Then decide, "Is it worth the time I will need to invest in order to see these changes?" I tell you today that

I speak from personal experience—Yes, it is worth the time! It will not happen overnight. People say that anything that changes needs at least 30 days to make a permanent change. That is the normal cycle, but if you stick to it, if you are willing and determined, *yes*—you will see a change!

Number 2 is home conditions. Along with the time it's going to take to make the changes, you need to make changes in your home. Right now:

- What is the foundation of your home?
- What is your home like?
- Who is in authority?
- What kind of atmosphere is in your home?
- Is there honor and obedience?
- What kind of words are you speaking?

These are all important things. Getting your house in order is an absolute must. You must be willing to make changes.

Number 3 is to change what you eat. We will go into this in depth in chapter 3

Number 4 is words. It is very important what words you are speaking over your children, over yourself, and over your circumstances.

- Are your words giving out positive or negative energy?
- Are you always speaking negatively and allowing others to speak negative words over your children?

You must be willing to change what you say. Words are powerful! Words have power. Power equals energy. Energy is needed in order to make the changes that need to be made. Again we will go into detail at a later time.

Number 5 is attention.

- How much attention are your children getting?

It is a known fact that children must have a certain amount of attention. If it is not being given in the home, then they will look elsewhere, but it doesn't matter if it is positive or negative attention. If we are not giving our children positive attention, then we wonder:

- Why are my children acting up in school?

Well, they are striving and hungering for love and attention. So another thing is:

- How many times a day do you tell your children that you love them?

Not just showing it by giving them stuff, but actually speaking it over them and saying, "I love you."These things are needed to change your home conditions. So we have talked about time, we have talked about home conditions, we have mentioned that what you eat is important, we have talked about words, and we have talked about love and attention. And that is how you can get started! Next we will talk about getting your house in order and establishing authority.

Notes

Challenges:

Goals:

What can I begin to do right now?

Chapter 2

Getting Your House in Order

The next thing that we are going to talk about is establishing authority. In getting your house in order, you must have authority.

- Who is running your house?

The word authority actually means the right to command and expect obedience.

- Are your children running your house?
- Are you running your house?
- Is someone else running your house?

Teaching your children obedience is important. To honor is very important. These again are things that must be established!

We are talking about getting your house in order. We have gone through some of the basic things needed. We have talked about how your authority is important. Now we are going to talk about the foundation of your home. My husband is a contractor. He builds homes or remodels older homes. And any builder will tell you that the most important thing—the thing they spend the most time on, the thing they make sure is the strongest and has the most elements put into it—is the foundation. The foundation of the home must be strong in order to hold up the walls and the roof. So they spend the most time on it. The bigger the house is, the stronger the foundation must be. It must be secured in several different ways. Well your foundation in your home is also very important. Having a foundation in your home is like the foundation in the building of a house.

- What is your basic belief system?

This absolutely must be established before you can go any further. The basic belief system or foundation of your home means:

- What *is* and what *is not* accepted in your home?
- What do you allow to go on?

Your children and everybody in your house must know what you believe. They must know what they are allowed to do, what they are allowed to say, how they are allowed to act and how they are not allowed to act, and what the circumstances (or the consequences) are when they don't act that way. This is very important in building a home. Again, if your foundation isn't established, the whole rest of the house will collapse. If builders just throw up a faulty foundation, using any kind of wood or any kind of cement, and just throw up any kind of beams and don't care if it is secure; when they start putting up the walls, that whole foundation is going to collapse because it has not been established and structured and secured in the correct way.

The next thing in the building of your home is the walls or structure. These are the things you do with your family to make your home run successfully. The rules that are followed are considered to be the structure. The foundation is your basic belief system: the structure is rules. Establish rules for your children with them. Write them down. Children can't remember—they have to be written down. We have our rules on the refrigerator and in their bedrooms. If you have several children in the home, younger children, older children, or teenagers, they all need to know what the rules are! It's very basic. They already know the basic belief system of your home, now what are the rules? What are they allowed to do? And according to the age of the children, the rules must be age-appropriate. A three-year-old would not have the same rules as a sixteen-year-old would have. So that's why everybody needs to know the rules and the consequences for breaking them. Having a structure also includes establishing times for chores, reading, and homework.

The roof provides finishing touches and a covering for safety. This means that you need to keep your children safe from outside forces. This is again very important. Children need to know that they are safe. They need to be able to come home—whether it is from school, or when they are older, from a date—knowing that they can look forward to the fact that when the doors are closed, they are safe in their house from outside forces. They need to know that the person in authority is not going to allow something into their house to disrupt it and make the children feel unsafe. This is very important! Parenting means to guide, guard and to govern: to train your children is to guide; to guard is to protect them; and to govern is to discipline and correct them.

Now let's talk about atmosphere. Four things determine the atmosphere of the home:

1. Music and television

- What do you allow your children to watch and listen to?

You must guard what they hear and what they see. We have five senses: ears, eyes, mouth, nose, and hands. What you touch, what you see, what you hear, what you taste—all go into your soul. What do you allow to go in there? If your children are constantly watching violent TV, hearing violent music, and being exposed to negative, negative things; that's what they're going to act out! What goes in is what will come out. If you allow that violent atmosphere to go on, and then your children act up, you need to look at that and say,

- Is it because of what they're watching and listening to?

2. Company and conversation.

This means guarding your words and who you let into your home. Again, we talked about how words have power. Power creates energy: energy is needed for force.

The same principle applies here:

- Who do you allow to come into your home and when they come in, do they know what is allowed in your home?

Everybody coming into your home should know your basic belief system. They should know what they are allowed to do in your home. Do not allow people to come into your home and just speak negatively over your children. Do not allow outsiders to come in and say whatever they want to say, or let them ruin the atmosphere of your home by bringing in any kind of music that they want or by bringing in any kind of video that they want. *You* are the guard or the authority of your home! You need to make sure that anybody coming into your home knows exactly what is allowed.

3. Quiet time or meditation.

Everybody needs quiet time in this busy world that we have. In our society the kids go to school probably 5-6 hours a day and parents have the hustle and bustle of work. Because of this, you need to have a time to come home and have a time of quiet or meditation. That should be a time where all the music, TV, or any kind of noise is shut off. And it may be a time when you can just sit and read or it may be a time that you can spend reading with your children. Or it may be a time that you just spend talking with your children, or it may be a time that you spend putting a puzzle together, or whatever. But there must be quiet time or meditation! That is a very important part of the change that needs to be made.

4. Vision of the home.

And last, but not least is the vision of your home. You need to write down your vision. Every family should have a vision so that they know where they are going.

- What is the future like?
- What are we striving toward?

You, your children, your husband, your family (whoever it may be) needs to know what the vision is.

There has to be balance in your home. There has to be love, acceptance, approval and affection. There also has to be authority for discipline and correction. This kind of home (which is ordered correctly) will stop the majority of the behavior problems that you are now having with your children. It will carry over into how they act in the classroom at school and also into how they treat those in authority when they are out of your home. It will make a difference and a change in their behavior because it's changing *the pattern of the behavior* in your child.

So again, I reiterate, when you ask, "How do I start?" Sit all the members of your home down and tell them, starting now: who's in authority; these are the rules; this is what is expected; this is what we believe in this house. Write them out and have them say out loud every day:

- I will obey the rules.
- I will love.
- I will do my chores.
- I will keep my home in order and peace.

Have them say, "I will", not what they will not do, not what they can't do, but what they *will do!* I guarantee that you will see a change in the pattern of the behavior of everyone involved, if you keep this up for 30 days. And once you see the change, it will be so exciting that you will want to carry on and make sure that it continues.

Next we will talk about establishing honor and obedience. Honor and obedience are a very important part of making changes in your home. Honor and obedience must work together. We are going to talk about what the word honor means and what the word obedience means and how we establish them. You must understand that your children must be honoring and obeying you because they want to and they respect you: not out of fear.

The word honor means to hold someone in high respect; to revere them; to speak highly of them or lift them up. Honor is an attitude—the way we think and believe about something determines how our life will go. If you think of different examples of honor; a "medal of honor" that the military gives out signifies that someone thought more about another person's life, revered them enough, respected them enough to put them before their own life. So they are recognized for honoring them and are given a medal of honor. Another example that may be closer to home is the Honor Roll at school. If you made the Honor Roll it means that you thought highly about education and respected the teacher's teaching. You tried to do your best and make them proud, so you were honored for your achievement: you were thought highly of. So in summing up, honor is when you think highly enough of someone to respect their wishes and commands.

- How do we instill honor in our children?

People ask me that all the time:

- How do you establish honor?

Number one you must be an honorable person—this means someone that they will want to honor. They must have watched you to see how you act. Then they will want to honor you. You have to honor people in authority. They are watching you to see how you treat people in authority. Your children watch you as an example—you are a living example. What do you do?

- Do you honor those in authority over you?
- Do you respect their commands?
- Do you obey them?

If your children see you constantly in rebellion against authority, then they're going to think that's okay. If they see you doing it, then they'll think it's okay to talk back to a teacher, or they'll think it's okay to talk back to a police officer, and they will usually rebel against you also. You need to teach your children about authority; you need to teach them to honor and obey the authority. Do not, under any circumstance, allow your children to be disrespectful or talk back to or say no to someone in authority.

Obedience is the action that works in and together with honor. *Obedience* means: to comply with or meet the command of. Children are to obey their parents quickly and quietly. You need to establish that there is a benefit to every obedience and a consequence for every disobedience. Establish what the benefits and the consequences are in your home, and make sure that your children understand them.

When teaching your children obedience, they must hear and value your words. They must respond to your voice the first time. They must respond to your voice at a conversational level, without you screaming at them. Don't allow a debate over obedience! Don't threaten, bribe or manipulate obedience out of your children. A strong-willed child will need you to be especially consistent, *consistent*, ***consistent!*** It will happen over time. Don't give up, don't lose control or become frustrated.

Your children might not obey you the first time if they don't understand what is being asked of them, if they honestly didn't hear you, or if they're afraid. So you have to begin training your children by making eye contact. When you speak tell them, "I want you to look at me." Tell them with your voice at a conversational level. Have them answer you by saying, "Yes, ma'am" or "Yes, sir." Our children say "Yes, ma'am" or "Yes, sir" to us, and that's how we know that they have understood us. Then they are expected to go and do it. It doesn't need to be repeated two, three, or four times, because they've understood and said, "Yes, Ma'am," therefore they are expected to go and do it. If they have any questions, they are to ask them at that time. If they say that they didn't understand it, then you repeat it for them.

I'm going to give you some steps that we actually took with our children when we first got them. At the ages of 4, 5, 6, and 7 they had a lot of issues and a lot of problems. The first thing we did was to sit everyone down at a table. (It could be anywhere as long as you include everyone in your house.) We, as the parents, made it clear that we were starting over again. Everything that they had done in the past was forgiven, and from that day forward there would be some new rules in our home. We, as the parents, said that "We are going to establish the authority and hang up the rules. We're going to start right now—clean from this day." We let them know that this was how we wanted our house to be run. This was what we expected of them. Everything in the past was forgiven; we were starting over. (It doesn't matter how old they are, if your children are 16 or 3 or 10 or a 4-year-old—it doesn't matter!) You can say, "We're starting over again and from this day forward changes are being made in our home. Everybody is going to change! These are the rules. This is what is not allowed in our home. This is what is going to happen if the rules are broken. This is how our house is going to be run. This is what is expected. And we, as the parents, are the ones in authority." Not our children; not another person living in our home, even if it is a relative; but "we the parents are the head of the household!" This goes for a single mom, husband and wife, or whoever is the head. "This is a new day, and this is where we are all starting right now." I promise you, that if you will keep this up, in thirty days you will see a difference!

Let's go back to the four things that are mandatory. It will take time! You must be willing

to invest the time. It's going to be making a change. You must be willing to change your

lifestyle! Recognize that what you are doing now isn't working or else you wouldn't be seeking help. You want to enrich your life and make it better and more productive. You want to find ways to enrich your family.

1. We're going to change our circumstances.
2. We're going to change what we speak. We're going to change our words over each other.
3. We're going to change the atmosphere.
4. And we are going to change ourselves.

And that is how we will get our house in order!

Notes

Challenges:

Goals:

What can I begin to do now?

Family Vision

Rules for Our Home

CHAPTER 3

What You Eat Matters

We have already talked about how to get started in Chapter 1 and about how to change your lifestyle. Now we will talk about how what you eat matters—nutrition, eating. Ask yourself:

- Does what you eat affect your mood and behavior?

What you eat does have a profound effect on several areas. In studying about nutrition, I read several books, did lots of research and attended seminars pertaining to the subject.

The reason I am sharing this is because of my own personal experience. We adopted four children (ages 4, 5, 6, and 7) of African-American descent. When we got them they had several issues. We had to deal with their problems in school: poor grades and study habits; lack of ability to concentrate or even focus; their low attention span; along with behavior issues. All of this caused them to be diagnosed as ADD and ADHD children with learning disabilities requiring the use of medication (or so they said) to function. This bothered me so much that I started researching—searching and reading and studying, because I needed to find some answers.

One area that I felt led to search out was about what they were eating. In the histories that we received when we adopted them, it was stated several times that they were undernourished and had been found left abandoned in the home without food. They were eating high amounts of sugar and junk food, or scraps of anything that they could find. Along with the other issues that we needed to address, we decided to change their diet—very drastically at first, cutting out *all* sugar.

In books I had read, I found that what you eat can have a profound result in several areas. These areas include: how you think; your intelligence level; your memory—what you can retain; your attention span; the amount of oxygen that reaches your brain; your mood and behavior—how you act and function throughout the day; the ability of brain cells to transmit messages; the level of nerve chemicals in the brain that regulate all mental processes; and the development and maintenance of the brain cells' function and structure.

What you are eating affects your energy level.

- How much energy do you have?

Negative energy pulls light energy out of your body. Fighting and arguing constantly in the home pulls energy away.

Poor nutrition and exposure to toxic drugs, such as narcotics and alcohol before birth or during birth, along with violence caused from too much TV violence, violent music, etc. which cause nightmares—all of these are well-known causes of A.D.D. and A.D.H.D.

Now let's look at the word nutrition. What does this actually mean? When I study something, I always like to look up words and define them to get a clearer picture in my mind of what they say. So we are going to look at poor nutrition vs. healthy eating. The word nutrition means the act or process of nourishing or being nourished, which means to create the growth of and repair the natural wastage of organic life. Organic life means the body organs—the life of the body organs. The word poor means: in bad condition, giving no birth to, producing nothing, lacking and inferior to. So lets put these two together—poor + nutrition = the lack of giving (no birth to), producing no nourishment which is needed for the growth and repair of our bodily functions. Wow! Isn't that a revelation? Therefore if a child is lacking nutrients, not growing or producing anything in his/her organs, how can a child be expected to function properly?

Poor nutrition would certainly have an effect on how they behave and how they think! The brain is not getting any nutrients and that affects their attention span—their body has no nutrients to function.

The foods we eat affect our emotional state. Being hungry causes your body to react. Your body will begin speaking to you in several ways, letting you know, "I'm hungry, I need food, I need nutrients!" It causes people to be cranky, crabby, emotional, fidgety and moody. We noticed a change in our children immediately when we changed what they ate and began feeding them healthy foods. They became calmer and more alert, their intelligence level improved and they began excelling at school. Again, I want to emphasize that this was a change concurrent with their change in the new environment that we talked about—a secure and stable home and time invested into them. I just want to emphasize that it is important that what you feed your children is directly related to their behavior and how they act. Again, the connections between food and mood are increasingly backed by research.

Here are some of the facts that I found while doing this research. They may really blow you away. The most direct way that food influences mood is, of course, its effect on blood sugar. Many people's moods deteriorate as their blood sugar level falls. The type of food eaten matters! *The type of food eaten matters!* I found when I was doing this research that there is a chemical in your brain that influences when and what you eat. It is called *serotonin*. It is the chemical in your brain that is also influenced by when and what you eat. It is a general mood regulator. It is a neuro-transmitter. No other neuro-transmitter is as strongly linked to your diet as serotonin. Whether there is a low or high level of serotonin in your brain will affect drastically how you feel and in turn affect your mood.

Low Serotonin Level	*High Serotonin Level*
1. Insomnia	1. Helps you to sleep
2. Depression	2. Will boost your mood.
3. Food cravings	3. Curbs food cravings.
4. Increased sensitivity to pain	4. Increases pain tolerance.
5. Unable to concentrate	5. Feel calm and alert.
6. Aggressive behavior occurs.	6. More passive behaviors.
7. Irritability, unable to concentrate.	
8. Poor body temperature regulation.	

Does any of this sound familiar? Passive (here comes another definition), as opposed to aggressive, means submitting or yielding without resistance or opposition. Submissive—wow! So you ask:

- What is the solution to boosting our brain cells?
- How do you keep the serotonin level high in the brain?

1. *You must take time to eat a healthy breakfast.* This is very important! People who eat breakfast think better and faster, remember more, react more quickly, and are mentally sharper than breakfast skippers. I want to take the time here to point out something that I have learned from working with children for many years and from my experience with my own children. My own children were used to grabbing a doughnut or a pop tart or some kind of a sugary food, and going off to school. A sugar high would boost their blood sugar level temporarily, but after ½ hour of being in school their serotonin level would begin to drop and they would not be able to concentrate. It affected their attention span and had a profound effect on them. So eating a healthy breakfast meant eating healthy—giving them whole-grain wheat toast, whole-grain cereal, pancakes, fruit juice, and fruits like fresh bananas, oranges or peaches. I always made sure that my children had some kind of fresh fruit before going to school. We will talk about the different kinds of food and why you should eat certain kinds of food at certain times of the day later on in the chapter. But for now, it is very important that you understand that you do not want to feed your children a huge amount of sugar. In fact, if you don't have to, it would be better not to feed them any sugar for breakfast or before going to school. They have slept all night long, for six or eight hours. They need to have something to stimulate their organs. They need to have something to stimulate their brain cells, to get the serotonin going. So they definitely don't need to be on a sugar high. That is the biggest factor that I observed when I volunteered in my children's classrooms several days a week was that if the students had not eaten a healthy breakfast, 10-15 minutes or half an hour after arriving at school they could not concentrate on their work, because their body was hungry.

2. *Choose a healthy snack vs. an unhealthy snack.* Again we will talk about what is healthy vs. what is unhealthy later on but of course, you know now that an unhealthy snack is any sugar booster, like doughnuts, cookies and cakes. A healthy snack would be cut-up vegetables and fruits, etc.

3. *Drink lots of water during the day.* Your body needs at least three to four glasses of water a day for maintenance.

4. *Prepare meals using fruits, vegetables, grains, etc.* Do not, again, let your children eat junk food all of the time. I realize that this is very hard, especially for single Moms that are working. I was fortunate enough to be married and able to stay home with my children for the first five years. So I made sure that I prepared meals and when they came home from school I prepared snacks so that they could have fruits and vegetables all the time. To stop at McDonald's after you have picked them up from the sitter or the "Y" or whatever, and grab them a hamburger, fries, and pop on the way home every day is going to definitely affect your child's behavior. They have to eat healthy meals!

5. *Avoid at all costs fats, oil, and sweets* as much as possible. The key word again is sugar, which causes a sugar high—try to avoid that by not giving it to them.

Now we are going to talk about which foods are healthy and which foods are not healthy and what time of day to eat them. Healthy foods give you a high level of serotonin and have a high-energy factor in them. Eating a snack in the middle of the day should be a food that is all natural. It must not be a protein-rich snack. Protein is found in meat and similar products. You want something that will boost your serotonin levels during the middle of the day, such as: fresh fruits and vegetables, carrot and celery sticks, nuts, etc. Eating a protein-rich food causes the amino acids in the blood level to rise. Amino acids compete for entry into the brain; therefore only moderate amounts of serotonin are made and stored. This leaves a person feeling depressed, irritable, tired, and craving. Their mood is one of tiredness; they are unable to concentrate or pay attention; they are irritable and feeling hungry.

Now let's look at the positive side. Eating a meal or a snack with natural carbohydrates causes the level of amino acids to drop as they enter the muscle cells. Therefore the serotonin levels remain high in the blood. This leaves a person feeling calm and peaceful, attentive and able to concentrate, and no longer feeling hungry. Their mood is more alert and energetic. So our conclusion is that eating a snack in the middle of the day must be a healthy natural snack and not a protein-rich snack. Once again the difference between proteins (found in Meat, sugars, etc.) as opposed to natural carbohydrates (fresh fruits and vegetables) is very important.

Your body needs fuel to function and the fuel for your body is food. At night most of your fuel is stored glucose. Most of the glucose reserves are drained by morning and you need a jumpstart. The jumpstart only comes from eating a natural carbohydrate meal.

- What happens when you skip breakfast?

Your body needs fuel to function. Fuel for your body is found in food (nutrients). Your body has been asleep 6-8 hours or more, causing your blood sugar level to drop. If you skip breakfast and do not refuel, this will occur:

- Skipping breakfast undermines your basic instincts.
- Fatigue and irritability occurs.

- You have poor concentration.
- You have muddled thinking.
- You will lack energy, be sluggish.
- You may be lethargic, with a state of indifference or excessive drowsiness.

A quick fix such as a doughnut or something with sugar in it only lasts an hour or two. Then your blood sugar drops again and you *never,* I emphasize, *never,* ***never*** regain the daylong energy you would have had if you would have taken the time to eat breakfast. You never make up for what you have lost.

Let's compare food to the gas in your car. They are both fuel.

- Do you have low energy, always feel tired and lack concentration or the ability to pay attention?

Look into how and what you are eating. Let's look at your car. You wouldn't expect your car to run on bad gas or go days without putting gas in your car. You would not neglect to check daily whether or not it needs gas—if you wanted it to function properly. You wouldn't expect your car to go or run on empty. Would you? Isn't your car very important to get you where you want to go, to get you through your day? It is very important for your daily activities. So then why would you think that your body could run right and function properly on anything but a quality fuel? The following things are absolutely essential: You must not skip breakfast. Eating too little early in the day causes all kinds of problems. Your body needs fuel to function! I am repeating this because it is important: your body has been asleep 6-8 hours—it has been that long since you last fed your body. If you go 6-8 hours and don't put gas in your car, or if you are going on a trip someplace and the tank beeps that it's empty, you are going to stop immediately and make sure that there is gas in it. Well you need to do this for your body. Eat a nutritious snack and drink lots of water. Do not fill yourself with proteins and sugar at lunchtime. Do not go on a quick weight loss diet that causes fatigue. Eat a well-balanced dinner, using all of the foods that we talked about: especially natural carbohydrates, which are fruits and vegetables.

- What are natural carbohydrates and how does your body use them?

First we need to define the word carbohydrate. The name means carbon + water. They are sugar compounds made by plants when the plants are exposed to light. The process of making sugar compounds is called photosynthesis, meaning light and putting together. Glucose is the sugar produced when you digest natural carbohydrates. Your body runs on glucose, the molecules that your cells burn for energy. Proteins, fat, and alcohol also provide energy in the form of calories. And protein does give you glucose, but it takes a long time for your body to get it. There are other ways that your body uses natural carbohydrates:

1. They regulate the amount of sugar circulating in your blood so that all of your cells get the energy that they need.
2. They provide nutrients.
3. They assist in your body's absorption of calcium.
4. They may help lower cholesterol levels and regulate blood pressure.

So you ask:

- Where do I get the carbohydrates that I need?

Number one, the most important sources of carbohydrates are plant foods, such as:

a) *fruits*
b) *vegetables*
c) *grains*

Let's go back to the original question:

- Does what you eat affect behavior and mood?

Children's behavior is constantly worse the morning after Halloween or any other sugar binge. Several teachers from my children's school where I was volunteering daily have told me that they can never understand why on the day after Halloween, when the children have been out Trick or Treating and have got a bag full of candy and are on a sugar high, that they can never get them to calm down and pay attention. They said that the entire day was ruined, that the children were all hyperactive, that they were running around on a sugar binge, and that they couldn't concentrate. Here is the reason why. Just a few hours after the sugar intake, children release large amounts of adrenalin, which causes them to experience the following:

A. Excitement—they are unable to sit still.
B. Shakiness—causing them to be fidgety.
C. Concentration problems.
D. Decreased ability to focus.
E. Anxiety

We can define metabolism as a chemical process that is constantly taking place in a living organism. It is the overall process of body chemistry. Any time that you take any kind of medication or drug, it alters the metabolism. It changes the chemical reaction, which in turn triggers a reaction in your body, affecting how you react. For instance, the reaction to emotion in active or strong-willed children will come out stronger and quicker than it will in passive children. A person's temperament and personality is also in the soul. So emotion triggering a reaction will take effect according to the child's personality and temperament. Any time you take any kind of medication or drug, it alters the metabolism. That's what it is meant to do. If your body is sick: if you have a fever, stomachache, headache, earache or whatever; taking medication is meant to alter the metabolism, to change the reaction. Most of the time it slows it down. Many times it makes you drowsy and causes you to want to sleep. When you are fighting a sickness or fever, this is good because your body, being in a relaxed state, helps your blood cells fight off infection. When you are active and running around it speeds up your metabolism. So we see that the human body, made up of many parts, plays an important role in keeping you healthy and in your right mind, thinking clearly. Unfortunately, there is also a negative side to taking medications or drugs.

Giving them medication for behavior problems has a down side. It only lasts for about 8 hours, and it only treats some of the symptoms. It provides short-term, superficial healing. And I wouldn't even call it healing. It is like taking a band-aid and putting it over a cut. You have covered it up, but when you remove the band-aid the cut is still there. It hasn't healed it, it has just covered it up so that you can't see it. The problem is still there, it only helps until the medication wears off. It does not treat the root of the problem: but causes side effects; appetite loss, insomnia, etc.; gets children into the habit of taking drugs or medication; and it may need to be taken throughout their life! It can be addictive.

Medication does not solve the problem; it just covers it up. When the medication wears off, the problem is still there. All that medication does is change the metabolism. A drug alters the state of your metabolism—it slows it down. As we defined metabolism earlier, it is a chemical process constantly taking place in a living organism. In order to keep behavior problems covered up or under control, when the medication wears off you need to give them more medication.

So my suggestion, which has been proven with my own children, is to change the way that they eat. What you eat matters! Get them eating healthy, off the sugar, and you will see a huge change in their behavior. It will definitely affect the way your children act, the way they think, the way their moods are, and the way that they behave. I guarantee that if you try this for 30 days, your life and your children's lives will never be the same again.

Notes

Challenges:

Goals:

What can I begin to do right now?

CHAPTER 4

Knowing Your Body and How it Functions

We will now begin talking about the body, the function of your body, and why it is very important to understand this. As you have seen before, I like to define words so that we know exactly what they mean. In *Webster's Dictionary* body means the main, central, or principle part of something. Function means the action for which a person or thing is especially fitted or used, or for which a thing exists. So lets put these two together and define body function. It means the main (central or principle) part that is acting for what it is designed to do. A person is made up of three parts: the spirit, the soul, and the body. What you put into your body does come out in some way. As the old saying goes, "What goes in must come out." Emotions have an effect on the body. What you eat has an effect on the body. So does what you hear and what you see. We're going to talk about metabolism and the five entrance points so that you understand how every part of your body works together. And if we are going to make the changes that are necessary, we must understand our body function and why it is so important to take care of it.

- What is metabolism?
- And what are the five entrance points?

Metabolism is a chemical process that is constantly taking place in a living organism. The five entrance points are: your eyes (what you see); your ears (what you hear); your nose (what you smell); your hands (what you touch); and your mouth (what you eat and say). Whatever you allow to go through those entrance points determines what is going to come out. The way a person conducts himself, his behavior, is determined through what is heard and seen, circumstances, words spoken, what is taught and also what has been eaten. Now I'm going to show you how this works.

When your metabolism is affected by something that has been put into it, it aggravates the whole body. It sends a signal to your head and you react in some way through the entrance or exit parts of your body—your arms, your legs, your mouth, your words, what you touch, what you see. For example, let's use this in regards to a child's behavior. The child who is constantly hearing violent music, seeing violent things on TV, and hearing violent words spoken over him and observing arguing and fighting in the home, has had their metabolism (chemical process in their body) affected. The adrenalin speeds up and goes to their head and in turn will come out in the way they act through one of their entrance points. It may come out as kicking or hitting, cussing and using bad words, fighting, or acting out in some way. The reason this is so important to understand is so that at an early age we can learn how to make the changes necessary for our children. We need to teach our children about emotions and how to handle them. This in turn will prevent a lot of the behavior problems that we deal with in our children. But we need to understand how the body works. This ties in with everything that we have been speaking about in other chapters. We have talked about food and how important it is that they are eating properly. We have talked about words and how important words are. I want to reiterate that this all goes together.

We need to talk more about metabolism and how it works. Because metabolism is the chemical process constantly taking place in a living organism (the overall process of body chemistry) it is very important to understand how it works. It could be compared to a demonstration in chemistry. When you put two certain compounds together that are compatible, you will get a positive result. But if you add something to them that is not compatible, you will get a negative result. The reaction will be totally different. So in comparison to our topic, any time you take any medication or drug, you are altering the metabolism—it changes the chemical reaction, which triggers a reaction in your body, which in turn affects how the person reacts.

For instance, in an active (or what I call a strong-willed) child the reaction from an emotion comes out stronger and quicker than in a passive child. A person's temperament or personality is located in their soul, which is something that we will talk about in the next chapter on understanding personalities and temperaments. So the emotion triggering the reaction will take place according to the individual child's temperament. But again, any time that you are taking any medication or drugs, you are altering the child's metabolism. It makes a difference. We talked about energy and what that meant and how it is going to come out of your body. It's very important to understand that any time that you take something that alters your metabolism, it alters in turn your body—the circulation of your blood, the function of your body, and in turn the reaction. Taking medication or a drug does not get to the root of the problem; it only changes what is going on temporarily.

- What happens when the medication wears off?

Think of this as an example. If a child gets a cut and is bleeding, and you take them and wash the cut and put a band-aid on it, the band-aid has covered up the cut. But the band-aid does not heal the cut; it only covers it up so that temporarily it is not bleeding. What happens when you take the band-aid off? The cut is still there! So your only choice is to put the band-aid back on again or else do something different. It is the same thing with a child on medication. You either have to give them more medicine, medicating them again to keep them in that sedated state or you have to begin to feed something different into them. What we are trying to teach you is that your alternative is to change the food and the words that are being put into them, which actually changes the problem, instead of just covering it up!

Now let's talk about emotion. The word emotion means: a strong surge of feeling that comes from the heart, which is based in your soul. When you have an emotion, it comes out of your soul, not your head. The soul is very passionate. It's the fuse that lights the fire to your feelings and emotions. So passion deals with your soul. The ability to express emotion is not learned; it is involuntary. So you did not have to learn how to cry, how to laugh, how to smile, or how to fear. It just came to you naturally. The way a person behaves or reacts to a situation is determined by what goes in him. Now that we understand about the body and how it works, we need to look at emotions and how it is important to learn how to control them.

- What does "healthy emotions" mean?

The word healthy means: free from defect or disease. Emotion means a strong surge of feeling. So healthy emotion would mean a strong surge of feeling that is free of defect and disease. Emotions like joy, laughter, cheerfulness, love, warmth, etc. are emotions that are responsive. They can change because they are affected by music, people, age, your physical condition, whether or not you are sick or upset, etc. They all stem from your soul—they are soulish emotions. The problems that you are having with your children are soulish or emotional. They are having an emotional reaction to a situation. One can be at peace when you have an appropriate response and you feel good about it.

For instance, in the discipline of a child, if they do not respond properly internally to the discipline, they will not be at peace, and there will be turmoil going on in their soul. That is just one example. We will be talking about this in another chapter.

- What happens when you live with healthy emotions?

When you live with healthy emotions (if your soul is healthy and you stay healthy in your body) there is an old saying, "Laughter is good for the soul". Why should we stay healthy? Our *soul* is the rational, emotional part of a man; the heart and the emotion of a man; personality, force, and essence of a man. If your soul and emotions are healthy, every other part of you—your mind and your body will be healthy also. They all work together!

- How do you react to situations?
- Are you a person who easily loses your temper?
- Do you get angry and throw things?

Let's talk about this. If your soul is all plugged up; if you have unresolved anger, hurt, frustration, hate, coldness, unforgiveness, then you are unable to express true love, joy, happiness, freedom, or laughter. This happens because our emotions are plugged up. No matter what someone has done to you—you have no control over their emotions—you do have control over yourself and over your children. In order to make room for healthy emotions to come through, you must rid yourself of unhealthy and unresolved issues: holding in hate, anger, bitterness and unforgiveness. Hate and anger turn to bitterness and unforgiveness.

- What do we need to do to unplug our emotions?

We need to walk in forgiveness. You need to release the person in your mind who has wronged you. Do not plot revenge. This keeps the unhealthy emotion alive. If you have to avoid them, that's fine. Don't allow yourself to become upset every time that you see a person that has wronged you. That will stop up all of your emotions.

Seize every opportunity to give encouragement. Encouragement is oxygen to your soul.

Do not respond to situations on impulse. Impulse means: to respond immediately to a strong emotion, with no regard to what is going to happen. Impulsive people act on how they feel, without ever thinking about it. If we don't understand about how our emotions function, then we become impulsive.

The reason we are talking about this is in regard to our children. For example, I will talk about our children. By now you know that when we adopted them they had a lot of issues and behavior problems. We immediately changed our lifestyle and their environment was radically changed. They were now in a secure and stable home with someone that loved them. We changed the way that they ate, we changed what was being spoken over them, and, of course, everything turned around. But we also had to sit them down at our family table and talk to them about the past. We had to say that as of this day we were starting over again. We must forgive whatever had happened in the past. We need to walk in forgiveness. We cannot hold that inside of us. You have to release whatever people harmed you or did wrong by you, whether it was voluntarily or involuntarily (whether it was meant or not meant). They may have been on drugs or something or they did not have the necessary knowledge of how to take care of you properly. But we had to actually speak out and say that:

- We forgive them.
- We are starting over from right now.
- We choose and purpose in our hearts to rid ourselves of all of that.
- We will put healthy words and thoughts, healthy food, healthy music and things that we hear and see into our lives.

And we did that. Our children did it one at a time and we did it as a family. And being able to forgive what has happened in the past is very important in the overall process of changing your lifestyle. We know that the reason we are searching and unhappy and frustrated with things the way they are now is because of something that has happened in the past. We cannot do anything about the past—we cannot control it. We all have issues and problems. We need to make sure that when we start with this new lifestyle, when we start applying these different principles that we have been talking about, that we start with a fresh mind, a fresh heart, and a fresh soul.

After saying all of that, I want to talk about your children for a minute. You need to learn how to channel their energy and steer them in the right direction. Help them to get their emotions under submission, by teaching them how to react properly to a situation and that they do not need to be given medication to slow them down or alter their behavior. We talked about how medication just covers it up and does not solve the problem.

When we talked about our human anatomy and how emotions affect our behavior, we talked about metabolism and what our body was meant to be and how it was meant to function. So when a drug or medication is put into our bodies, it alters the way that our body was originally meant to function. All I'm saying is that through all of the research that we did—numerous hours of study through books, on the internet, in seminars, what I heard and learned for myself and what I meditated on—all of this study taught me that your body is meant to function in a certain way. You were made a certain way. And the food that you eat, the words that are spoken over you, and the way that you react to situations all have to be done in a natural state. And that is what we are trying to talk about in this chapter—knowing your body: understanding how it functions; and understanding how important it is to keep your body clean, the blood flowing the correct way with your mind thinking the right thing, and your soul unplugged from unforgiveness, anger, hurt, unresolved issues; and your body metabolism working the way that it is meant to be without it being altered. That is the goal of this chapter.

In chapter 5 we will continue by talking about words and how words affect your body. Are your words producing positive or negative energy?

Notes

Challenges:

Goals:

What can I begin to do right now?

CHAPTER 5

Words Are Powerful

In Chapter 1 we talked about getting your house in order—how to get started and the things that you need to do to begin. In Chapter 3 we talked about how what you eat matters—how important it is to eat healthy in order to produce the behavior and the effect that we are looking for in our children and the change that we are expecting in ourselves and in our lifestyle. You must remember that these changes are not going to happen overnight. We must learn to change our lifestyle, we must learn to do it on a consistent basis, to be patient and wait and follow through for at least 30 days. And I guarantee that you will see the results that you are looking for.

We have been talking about ways to enrich your life. We have defined the word enrich and stated what it means. Obviously, because you are reading this, then you must be desiring a change. You are desiring a change in the behavior that you are seeing in your children, a change in the way you are living right now, a change in what is going on in your home. We have talked about getting started with honor and obedience and establishing the authority in your home in order to get your house in order. Now you are here and we understand that you are frustrated, maybe even at your wit's end. Perhaps your children are on some kind of medication. You may have been told by a teacher or someone else that your child cannot behave properly without the medication. But you are here reading this book to learn how to turn your situation around. In this chapter we are going to be talking about words. First and foremost, you need to know that what you are saying—your words—produce some kind of effect. You need to look at them and say:

- Do the words that I am speaking have any power?

Words are powerful. They can have either positive or negative power, but they do have power. Power is needed to produce energy.

Energy + Power = Force.

And if your words have no power and are falling on deaf ears, then they are not effective.

First let's define what we are talking about.

- How would you define "words" or "words spoken"?

Webster's Dictionary says that words are: 1) a communication or message sent forth; 2) a command, signal, or direction; 3) conversation, talk or remarks. Words produce energy—energy is needed for power. Let's put this together. Words or words spoken are defined as a communication or message sent forth.

- Is the communication or message that you send forth producing anything?

- Is the command, signal or direction that you are giving producing anything?
- Are the results what you want them to be or not?

If you had to answer "no" to any of these questions, let's look at why. We said that the words you are saying and how you are saying them do have an effect. They do produce energy, energy that is needed for power. If you have no energy, and if you have no power, that means that you have no force. And therefore what you are saying is not effective.

Let's take a minute to talk about energy.

- What is energy?

Energy is the special power that makes force. Force is the push and pull that makes something move. You have heard the word energy used many times. Sometimes people use it to describe how they feel. "I don't have any energy today." In science, energy has a special meaning. It's not something that we can see or feel or that moves, it is the measure of how much work can be done. Whenever we push or pull something that moves, we are doing work. When we do work we use energy. Whenever your body moves, you use energy.

Let's look at the different kinds of energy. There are three kinds of energy—kinetic energy, potential energy, and synthetic energy. First we are going to talk about kinetic energy.

- What is kinetic energy?

It is the energy of motion. It means to set something in motion. For example, your words set something in motion when you speak. You can choose to have it be something negative or something positive, according to what you say. If you speak negative things over your children all of the time, then that is what you are setting into motion and your children will respond negatively. If you speak positive things, then that is what you set into motion. Children will react to whatever is being spoken over them. Your words set something into motion, whether it is negative or positive. An example of speaking negatively is somebody who is constantly saying things like, "You are so stupid! You never do anything right. What is the matter with you? You can't control yourself, you are always acting up." Those words have just gone into the air, they have just come over your children. If your children receive them, then that is what they start to believe. "I'm so stupid. I can't control myself. I'm always acting up." And that is the result that comes from negative words.

Now let's reverse that.

- I know that you are smart.
- I know that you can control your emotions.
- I know that you can sit still.
- You are a smart person and you have the ability to sit and listen and obey.

If you say that over and over again to your children, they will begin to believe it. They will receive it and it will get inside of them. Before you know it, they will be acting it out. "I'm smart. I can sit still. I am capable of learning. I am capable of listening and obeying." And that is the result that you will get from speaking positive words. So again, you have the choice.

- What do you want to set into motion?
- What do you want your words to accomplish?

- What are you looking for (the end result) in your children?

Look at yourself and listen to what you are saying and begin to think about it.

Next we are going to look at potential energy. Potential energy is energy that does not move. Potential energy is stored up until it is used. For example, your muscles have potential energy while you are asleep and they are not in use. If you lift a heavy book high up in the air, you use energy to do it. The energy does not vanish; it remains in the book as stored energy called potential energy. If you release the book you are holding up in the air, it falls. That is the energy that is released—potential energy. The bow of a bow and arrow has potential energy. The archer does work to pull back the bowstring and the energy used is stored up in the bent bow. When the archer lets go of the string, the energy is released and shoots the arrow through the air.

Let's compare this with words that are spoken. You use energy to speak out words. They go forth into the air and your children absorb them. Even though you can't see them, they are stored up until such as time when they are released. So it is important to watch what you are saying. For example, when you wake your children up in the morning, if you are running behind, you are yelling and screaming—using a whole lot of energy (negative energy). You may be saying over your children, "Come on! Come on! We're going to be late! This day is starting off bad. You are always making us late. You're going to get to school and not be able to do anything. You're going to be late! What is the matter with you?" Those words have got into your children as stored up energy. They get into the car and get to school. When they sit down at school, they start thinking about those words. They may start to react to what was said over them and start to get frustrated and upset. That is what you have set into motion for the day.

I want to give you an example from my personal experience. On some mornings I get up and haven't had time to get my quiet time, or have not had time to spend drinking my coffee and getting my thoughts together, or whatever it may be. Nevertheless, I make sure—I purpose in my heart and make sure—that before my children go to school, after they have had a healthy breakfast, after we have taken time to have our quiet time together, (it may be a time of meditation, reading, or studying of spelling words, etc.), that before my children leave the house I say something positive over them. Or if I am driving them to school, before they get out of the car I purposely, every single day, say to them:

- You are going to have a great day today. Have a great day!
- I love you. You know how much I love you!
- You know how great I think you are—that you are smart and talented.
- Something great is going to happen today!

Those are just examples of something positive to say. I make sure that they do not enter into their school day or go into the school on a negative note, no matter how I am feeling. After they have got out of the car I may let out a deep breath or scream or give a sigh of relief because it has been a rough morning (since I have four children to get ready). Every morning isn't perfect. Maybe the alarm clock didn't go off, or you are just running behind. You may have purposed that today was the day to have that great breakfast that you had all planned and it just didn't work out. Those days happen.

Do not allow that to get on your children. If you are wanting to see a behavior change in your children, you need to really work at what you are saying over them. The last thing that they hear before they get out of your car, or before they are sent to the bus stop, or before they walk to school, or just before they run out the door, should be a positive remark. Try this as I can guarantee you from my personal experience that you will begin to see a change in how your children respond and react during the school day.

The last kind of energy is synthetic energy. Synthetic energy is described as energy produced artificially by chemicals, rather than occurring naturally. Wow, this is powerful. As described by *Webster's Dictionary*'s scientific definition of synthetic energy (I will repeat it again): *synthetic energy is energy produced artificially by chemicals, rather than occurring naturally.* I will touch on this later on in the book. Right now we are talking about words—power, energy, and force.

- What is power?

We have talked about words and what they mean, how words produce energy and what energy means, so now we are going to tell you how energy is needed for power. I want you to really get into this so that you can understand again how important what you say is. The word power means:

1) strength or force actually put forth
2) any form of energy available for doing work.

Powerful means: strong, possessing great force or energy. Definitions include:

a) exercising great authority,
b) having a great effect on the mind.

Wow! Powerful is exercising great authority. Does that sound familiar? Having a great effect on the mind—Your words should be powerful! You should exercise great authority and have a great effect on the mind of the person that you are speaking to. Power means strength or force put forth, which means that your words should be forceful and make things move. The tongue has the power of life and death. What you say over your children—your words—either bring life to them or death. For out of the overflow of the heart the mouth speaks. We've talked about this—if all that you have in you are negative things, that is what is going to come out of your mouth and in turn go into your children, then you will reap what you sow. Your children will in turn speak out what is in them. And if it is negative, that is the way they will speak and act.

Now let's look at the word force and talk about that along with the word momentum.

- What are force and momentum and how do they work?

Force is the push and pull that makes things move. Force is the push or pull that can make an object move or change direction! Force is also the push or pull that can make an object change the speed at which it is moving. Momentum means: the quality of motion in a body, measured by its mass and velocity or speed. The way it works is that force is needed to stop any object in motion (for example, a car—because a car has momentum). If a car is moving at a high speed, it has more momentum that it would have while moving at a slower speed. For this reason, a greater force is needed to stop a fast-moving car. Let's compare this with our words that are spoken. Words produce energy, and energy is needed for power. Force is the push and pull that makes some kind of energy move. The less energy you have, or if you have no energy, then you have no power.

- What happens when you have no energy?

Screaming and yelling uses a whole lot of energy. Remember when we talked about the potential energy that your body has stored up? When you yell or scream, hit, kick, or shake your body in every possible way, that uses up all of your stored energy and causes the body to be in a weakened stage, and therefore you lose power and are ineffective. Your words used by screaming and yelling go into the atmosphere and are usually shut off by the party listening. They fall to the ground and die, and are therefore of no use. We talked about how the tongue has the power of life and death. Well here is a case where your words have died and you have produced absolutely nothing, accomplished no goal, changed nothing by what you said (or yelled and screamed). You have managed to wear your body down, losing energy and power, causing you to become weakened and tired.

- What happens when you speak positive words combined with energy and power?

Positive words are words of encouragement. Encouragement is oxygen to the soul. When we speak positive words of encouragement with energy and force, which in turn produces power, we are actually changing something in the atmosphere. Even though you cannot see it, it enters into your child's soul through the entrance points we told you about. Positive energy pushes out the negative. To review, the entrance points are what you see, what you hear, what you feel, what you speak and what you smell. These are the entrance points where things come into your children. Again, things enter in through what they hear, what they see, and what they speak or what is spoken over them, and what is touched. Positive energy then pushes out the negative. Then in turn, it causes a positive result.

- Where do you get energy?

First and foremost, people get energy from healthy foods. Your body digests or breaks down food into energy. Food becomes the power that allows your muscles to push and pull. Certain foods like junk food have no value. Eating a lot of junk food will result in no energy. Eating healthy foods like vegetables, fruits, nuts, and grains are important in order for your body

to maintain energy. Junk foods are usually high in calories from sugar and fat and very low in most nutrients. All of the earth's energy comes from the sun. The sun has a very big supply of energy. It gives its energy through sunlight to the plants. Plants grow and pass that energy along to the animals and people who eat them. For example, eating a juicy peach is a great way to give our body energy. The peach tree uses the sun's energy to grow and make the peach. The sun gives some of its energy to the peach tree. And the peach tree passes the energy on to us in the peach that we eat. So as you can see, it is essential that we eat healthy foods in order to have energy, which in turn gives us power, which is the force that generates the words we speak. The words we speak then bring a result on the behavior of our children.

Now let's look at four questions to answer:

1) Do your words accomplish what you want them to?
2) Are your words powerful in a positive or negative way?
3) Do your words have force?
4) Do your children obey your words the first time you speak?

In order to answer yes to all of these questions, you must be doing the following:

1. **Speak boldly in a normal tone of voice after first** getting your children's attention by making them stop and look at you. For example, when we want to talk to our children we do not yell up to the top of the stairs for them to come down. We do not run through the house. We call our children and make them come and stand in front of us (about a foot in front of us). We make them make eye contact and speak in a normal tone of voice. We give the command—we don't ask it in a question form e.g. "Will you please do this"—we present it as a command.

   - This is what I want you to do.
   - Go and clean your room.
   - Do you understand?

   It is in a command form. We make them acknowledge that they heard it, repeat it, and then answer by saying, "Yes Ma'am" or "Yes, sir." We spoke about this in Chapter 1 in regards to honor and obedience.

2. Give commands in a positive manner, not saying what they should not do, but rather what they *should* do. For instance, if your children are fighting and arguing, and you don't want them to do that, you do not yell at them and say, "Do not argue and fight anymore!" You walk in and say:

- I want you to start speaking positive words.
- I want you to say something kind (for young children)
- I want you to ask your brothers and sisters "May I play with you?"

So you reverse it and make sure that your command is presented in a positive way.

3. While you're speaking, make sure that your children are looking at you and have acknowledged what you have said.

4. Make your children do what you have said quickly and with the right attitude. Again we talked about that in our chapter on honor and obedience.

Follow all of these steps, along with eating healthy so that you will have energy, which all ties together with all that we have talked about in the previous chapters, and speak in a normal tone of voice (not yelling and screaming so as to lose a lot of energy which you have stored up). Knowing that you need energy in order to have power will cause the words you speak to be powerful and you will see a difference in your children's behavior. Again, I am speaking from personal experience and have given you examples of how we dealt with our children and I can tell you that we have seen a huge change in their behavior from the time that we first got them.

The last thing I want to talk about is synthetic energy. I want to explain how this kind of energy is different than the other two kinds, and about the effect that it has when you give your children something that alters their metabolism chemically. I want to describe synthetic energy and how it works. Synthetic energy is energy produced artificially with chemicals rather than being produced naturally. What does this mean? Well, as we have touched on, any time that you take drugs or medication of any kind, it alters your metabolism, which is the chemical process constantly taking place in a living organism. Taking drugs or medications alters this: it changes the chemical reaction, which in turn triggers a reaction in your body that affects how you react. We already said that you need energy for power. Whenever your body moves you use energy. If you have no energy, you will have no power.

So if you have altered your metabolism by the use of drugs or medication and it has changed the chemical reaction, then in turn you have altered the kind of energy that you are producing. It is no longer natural energy, but synthetic energy—energy produced artificially by chemicals, rather than occurring naturally. Your body is still producing energy, but it is going to be in a different form. All of those chemicals going into you will have to come out in some form. But when the energy produced comes out, it is uncontrolled, and being uncontrolled it has no power. You cannot direct it where you want it to go. Just as we have talked about negative emotions, negative words, and negative things in your soul will be what will come out; it is the same way with energy. People get energy from healthy foods. Constantly putting junk food into your system turns to sugar and fat, as stated before. It is of no use. It is the same thing when you are constantly putting chemicals and medication into your body. It is of no use as far as energy goes, and therefore has no power. Let's go back to talking about our children. Constantly giving them medication does not get to the root of their behavior problem, it only alters their metabolism. It slows it down long enough for them to be in a sedated state, which may seem controlled. But when the medication wears off, because you have produced artificial energy and it has no place to go but out, your energy has no power and comes out uncontrolled.

- What can we do when our child is taking medication and that energy comes out uncontrolled?

  There are only two things that you can do:

1. Sedate them again, keeping them on the medication.
2. Change what you are feeding into them, feeding naturally through what they eat and the words that are spoken over them.

What your child hears and what they eat has a huge effect. So you need to look at yourself and ask yourself: "What am I trying to do here?" If you want your child's behavior to change for the positive, if that is what you want to accomplish, then you need to start looking at changing your lifestyle—putting healthy foods into them, speaking the right words over them, changing the way you run your household, in order to see a different result.

I repeat that your words have power—is it positive or is it negative power?

- What do you want to accomplish with your words?
- What do you want your end results to be?
- Do you want them to be powerful in a positive or negative way?

Feeding our children two things in a natural state—***healthy foods and healthy words***—will make a difference! I promise you and I speak from experience that you will see a change if you continue on and do not give up!

Notes

Challenges:

Goals:

What can I begin to do right now?

Chapter 6

Understanding Temperaments and Personalities

It is very important to understand that everyone is different. No two people are alike, nor are your children. When you understand your personality, what you are like and what your strengths and weaknesses are; that helps you to better understand your children and how to react and handle how they behave.

- What is personality?

Webster defines personality as: the distinctive qualities or characteristics of a person. Distinctive means: different than others; unlike; not the same; separate. Qualities means: elements or the nature of something. Characteristic means feature or trait. So lets redefine personality now by putting these all together as: separate element, feature, or trait of a person. Personalities fall into two categories.

- What are the two categories of personalities?

They are: 1) extrovert or active
2) introvert or passive

Extrovert or Active	*Introvert or Passive*
Energized	Laid-back
Outgoing	Slow
Fast	Low-paced
Spontaneous	Sets Boundaries
No Boundaries	Directs attention & energy inwardly
Directs attention & energy outwardly	

- What are the personality traits of a strong personality?

The *Active* person is a person that is an organizer. They are very innovative, place a high value on time, and are always challenging the status quo. Their weakness is that they are likely to overstep authority, they don't like routine, are argumentative, and their greatest fear is being taken advantage of. They are strong-willed and will have to be handled differently than a passive child or one that is compliant. They are leaders, self-reliant, and take risks. They like handling multiple projects and welcome Challenges without any fear. They can overcome obstacles and function well with a lot of things to do. They are willing to speak out and provide direction. They are usually optimistic and they make great leaders.

The *Extrovert* or creative problem-solver is also a great encourager. They are a peacemaker and don't like to get into controversy. Their possible weaknesses would be an over-concern with popularity, being inattentive to detail, the tendency to overuse gestures and facial expressions, and the tendency to listen only when it is convenient. They also fear rejection. You need to look and see what kind of child you have.

We have two very active children and two passive children. Because we know this, we have to handle them differently. Our Active and strong-willed children mainly have to have consistency, *consistency*, and ***consistency***! Of my passive children, my little girl will repent and ask forgiveness if she hears loudness in my voice and even thinks that I am upset with her. She doesn't need a lot to get her going because she is very sensitive and she handles things differently. So it is very important for you to understand the differences in their personalities.

It is very important that you understand what your children are like, but you first have to understand what *you* are like and what motivates you.

- What is your personality?
- Are you a laid-back person or are you an Active person?
- Do you take a lot of chances?
- Are you a high risk-taker?

You need to understand this before we get into our chapter on how to discipline your child with creative discipline.

We are also going to be talking about temperament. Temperament is different. It is the way that you think about something. It is very important that we understand the difference in these. If you are a person who is always a risk taker, always going after something, and you challenge the status quo, that will make a difference in the way that you respond to your child's behavior. Temperament is defined as the way you think or gather information causing you to act. So temperament is the way you think that causes you to act a certain way that is known as your personality.

There are two ways that you gather information, or two kinds of temperaments. The type of temperament determines what you use to make decisions.

Sensing or Intuitive	*Thinking or Logical*
Feeling	Thinking
Emotion	Logic
Usually women	Usually men

So it is important to understand the difference in temperaments, even between a male and a female. If you have girls in your home vs. boys in your home, you must know that girls are going to make decisions (most of the time) based on how they feel about something. They are going to react with their emotions, while boys are going to base their decisions on how they think about something. That is important to understand.

You might want to try this perception test. Put out a glass of water that is filled halfway. Ask your family members: "Do you see this glass as half full or half empty"? This will give you an idea of how they view things. If you are an optimist or positive person, you will see it half full. If you are a pessimist or a negative person, you will see it half empty. This is important to know.

We will talk more about temperaments later. Now we will go back to talking about personalities. If you have a very Active or strong-willed child, you need to really watch when you are speaking to them, because they like to be controlling and domineering. They are not very good listeners. We have two children that are very Active or controlling so we have to really make sure that we get their attention, focusing on eye contact, and making sure that they are not talking. One of my daughters has many times wanted to monopolize the conversation—when I am talking to her, she wants to put her two cents worth in. So I have to stop and say: "Close your mouth, you are not going to speak when I am talking, you are going to listen." And you are really going to have to work on them becoming a listener, because that is not one of their strong points.

Active children are sometimes hard to approach. Sometimes people will look at them and think that because they are so Active, and so defiant to authority at times (because they always want to be in charge) and they may be a hard person to befriend because of this. You don't want to put two Active personalities together, because they will both want to take charge. In my household, when we got our children, my four-year-old girl definitely dominated her eight-year-old sister because the older girl had a passive, easy-going, "don't want to rock the boat" type of personality. The younger one had learned over the years that she could dominate her brothers and sisters. So it is very important that you try and channel those different personalities in the way that you want them to go, because if you don't, when they get older that Active, domineering, controlling personality will only get stronger and it will be even harder to approach and deal with. This is one of the areas that we had to work on and are still working on, quite honestly.

Active personalities are great leaders and will definitely be the one to pick if you want to get something done, as opposed to someone that is laid-back, because they will definitely take on a challenge and handle it. They are very good in a crisis. They are very good as far as providing direction and leadership, but they are not always very supportive of other team members. They always like to be in charge and don't always appreciate the value of other people's opinions, feelings, or desires. These things will be important to remember when we talk about the chapter on discipline, because you are going to go about the way you discipline the children—I am not talking about the rules in your house—but in approaching them, you will handle it differently when you are disciplining a strong-willed or Active child than you would a passive child. That is why we are getting into this area of personality and understanding it.

Another demonstration of temperament is the following demonstration. Hold up a doll or toy that has one arm missing. Then ask whether you see the negative or the potential. If you are a pessimist, you will say, "Oh my goodness, she's missing an arm—how awful!" and will go into all the reasons that it is so terrible that her arm is missing. That's all that you focus on, you have immediately gone to the problem. But if you are an optimist or different type of personality, you are going to look at the whole doll and see the potential and not direct your eyesight to the problem. Just like the glass that is half full or half empty, what are you looking at? Do you see it as half full or half empty?

- Are you focusing on the problem, or what you don't have?
- Or are you focusing on the potential, or what is already there?

And again that relates to personality and temperament. I want to reiterate the difference between temperament and personality. We defined temperament as the way you think or gather information, causing you to act. It could also be defined as the physical and mental peculiarities of an individual. So temperament is the way you think which causes you to act a certain way, known as your personality. The way you think has a whole lot to do with the way you act, your perception! Why am I stressing this talking about personality and temperament? Don't you see the relationship again, that the way you think about something—be it positive or negative—the way that you perceive something (the perception of half empty or half full, the potential or the problem) has a direct affect on the way that you behave or your personality.

All of this ties into everything that we have been talking about from the beginning, or our focus. If you stop and understand, it all has an affect on the way that you behave, or your personality. If you start to understand what kind of personality that you have and ask yourself:

- What are my strengths?
- What are my weaknesses?
- Do I fear rejection, or being taken advantage of, or that someone will take over?
- What am I like?

I myself know that I have a strong personality and that I am a dominant person. I have those strong dominant characteristics and so I have to watch when it comes to raising my children, especially in the area of discipline that we are going to talk about. Knowing yourself—knowing your body, knowing what you think, and knowing how you act—knowing yourself will help you to better understand your children. And my main goal was to better understand my children, especially since I had not birthed them and they were adopted, I needed to know as much about them as I could. And I had to change some things myself; I had to be willing to do that in order to see a change in my children. So personality and temperament are important and the more that you understand it in yourself, the better equipped you will be to handle your children.

CHAPTER 7

Creative Discipline

Now we are going to talk about creative discipline.

- What is creative discipline?

First we will define it so that we will have a clear understanding of what we are talking about. Discipline is defined in *Webster's Dictionary* as: the training of the mental, emotional and physical powers of a person by instruction, control and exercise. Discipline is also defined as training that develops self-control, character, order, and efficiency, which are productive results.

Every child must understand that there is a consequence for every disobedience and a reward for every obedience. Now let's define correction vs. punishment.

- What is correction?

Correction is defined as a change that corrects a mistake, a change from wrong to right, a change from abnormal to normal. Love must be the only motive for discipline and correction. Now let's define punishment.

- What is punishment?

Punishment is defined as a penalty imposed for a crime or thought committed with the intent to inflict harm or pain. The difference between discipline and punishment is: Discipline is the training and instruction to produce productive results, whereas punishment is penalizing by inflicting on the fault without producing any change. Wow—what an eye-opener!

Now let's define creative discipline and explain how it works. The word creative means to originate; come into existence by originality of thought and execution. Discipline is training that develops self-control, order and efficiency with productive results. So let's put those together. Creative discipline is: bringing into existence a means of training that will develop self-control, order, and efficiency with productive results. Our ultimate goal is to alter behavior patterns from negative behavior to positive behavior.

- So how do we begin to train our children to behave properly and make right choices?

The first thing we do in training a child is sit them down and help them to understand about rewards and consequences—the fact that there is a consequence for every disobedience and a reward for every obedience. Start by defining the rewards and consequences. Children need to have explained very plainly what is expected of them and what is not acceptable. Do not assume that your children know!

- What are rewards and consequences?

Reward means something given or done in return for an act, service or achievement committed. Note:

Rewards are not the same as bribes. Bribe means an attempt to influence behavior, usually when dealing with someone who has no moral value. Apply rewards by using a system, for example, in our house we use a point system. They earn points for right and appropriate attitudes and behavior. I have a chart on the refrigerator. I have all of the things that are expected of them; including chores, attitudes, homework, and behavior (like we talked about in the chapter on Getting your House in Order). They just have to come home and look at the chart. We don't have to have a huge debate or screaming session over it, they just have to look at the chart. If they have done what they were supposed to do correctly and with the right attitude, at the end of the day they will get a point, or you could use stickers, stars, etc.

Another way is to win so much free time, or time spent alone with your parent or guardian. Or you can have a reward bucket or jar with cards in it that are worth so many points. An example would be that your child has earned 10 points at the end of the week. You would allow them to pick out of the 10 point bucket with cards like 10 points=$1 to spend at the Dollar Store or one hour to spend alone with Mom and Dad. During that hour they might be able to go shopping, or just sit down and play a game. That to children is very important, especially if you have a large family like ours with four adopted children. To them it is very important to have a special time with Mom and Dad. Even though we often take the whole family and go someplace, they love to have that individual attention. Or sometimes we will have a girls' day or a boys' day. Maybe the girls get to go and get their nails done or their hair or whatever it is—it's a reward for having the proper behavior that we want during the week. And this is the way that kids will start doing and responding the way that you want them to, as you reward them in a positive way. And when they don't—we'll talk about consequences in a little bit and what that means.

Rewards can include even simple things like praise and validation, encouragement, affection, time spent, or special gifts and surprises. Buy them something special or fix their favorite meal. A special gift could be a plaque, or something that is especially just for them—like a poem that you wrote. One time I sent a bouquet of flowers to the school that my daughter was attending. I left them at the office and they delivered them directly to her homeroom where she was and you wouldn't believe the responses that she got when they delivered them to her. Even some teachers and the principal came up to me and said that it was so great and it had really boosted her self-esteem and encouraged her.

Even to this day my son treasures one of the things I gave to him when he had done something that really pleased me and I really wanted him to continue in that behavior. That is why you reward them, because you are telling them:

- I just really loved the way you have behaved and that is the way I want you to continue behaving.
- You really made a great choice.

Especially when they are going through a tough time or a time when they may even be under peer pressure and they made a good choice that you are pleased with, then reward them at that point and really praise and encourage them so that they will continue in that behavior. They will realize that the choice they made caused Mom and Dad (or guardian or relative) to be really pleased with them. My son at age 13 still has the little teddy bear that he named "Cinnamon" and he'll say,

"Remember, Mom, when you brought this to the school and you were hiding in the coatroom, and they brought it into the classroom and then my teacher had you come out and how exciting it was?" At the time he may have looked embarrassed or whatever, with his head down, but believe me—it meant a lot to him. So there are all types of rewards.

Now let's talk about consequences. Consequences can include the following: discouragement, loss of approval, or disappointment. Disappointment means letting your child know that you are very unhappy with them. Let me talk about this is relationship to temperament.

I have two strong-willed children and two passive children. For us to be discouraged or upset with my one passive daughter is just devastating to her. For me to say to her, "I am really upset with you, I really disapprove of what you did today, and you have disappointed me greatly," just devastates her because she really strives to win our approval and she is very quick to repent and say that she is sorry. She will go to her room and cry and cry and sometimes almost immediately she will come down and say, "I am so sorry, Mom, will you please forgive me? I know that I made a bad choice." And she needs that "OK, I forgive you" and the approval of hearing me say that I still love her, but I am not happy with her behavior. For the next few days she just strives very hard to change her behavior around and when the same situation comes up again, she is quick to make the right choice, because she does not want to experience our disapproval again.

Now in a strong-willed child you may have to handle it differently, like giving them a loss of privilege, taking away something that they enjoy. It could be a loss of the time that you were going to spend with them. With our strong-willed children (we have one son and one daughter who have very, very dominant personalities) you will have to handle them differently. They like special gifts and time spent alone. My daughter likes to go and get her nails done or have a girls' day. So we may have to take away something that they really like. We have had to replace something that they like with something that they do not like.

For example, my son absolutely cannot stand sauerkraut. For the first year or so when we were really trying to train him, we worked with his teacher and when he would act up in his classroom, he would be given sauerkraut. This was allowed because we were not withholding food from him, we were just replacing something that he liked (like pizza) for lunch and would have him eat the sauerkraut instead. At first the teacher would call us and his Dad came from work and sat in the lunchroom eating our son's lunch while he had to eat the sauerkraut. After about three times of him misbehaving and realizing that his Dad would come to the school, all the teacher had to do was hold up a can of sauerkraut and say, "Michael, do I have to call your Dad to come and feed you this for lunch?" and he would straighten right up. Now, of course, this won't work if it is not feasible for you to take off of work and come to the school. You have to choose a consequence that you will be able to follow through on, because if they call your bluff, then you will have to be able to do it. Watch what you commit to and say because you do not want your words to not be true.

We have touched on some examples of how to apply rewards and consequences. Let me remind you again that rewards are not the same as bribes. We do not want to use bribes. Don't say to your child, "If you behave yourself in the grocery store, I will buy you a candy bar." That is a bribe. It means that the only reason they are behaving is to get a candy bar. That is not why we want our children to behave. We have talked about honor and obedience. We want them to behave and make right choices because they are doing it out of honor for you and obedience. So don't use a bribe.

We apply rewards using a system—a point system, free time, stickers, bags with points, etc. Another thing that we have done in the past is to have six or seven lunch bags loaded up with points on the outside of them (3, 5, 10, 20). At the end of the week they got the bag with the number of points that they had earned that week. The child with the 3-point bag may have noticed that the child with the 20-point bag had a $20 bill in his bag while his had only 3 stickers. That did not go over very well. If they said "That's not fair!" We replied that, "you all had the same chance to earn points. By the end of the next week, if you get that many points, you can earn this one too." If you have several children in the home they will be able to see that you made it equal. It wasn't that anyone was rewarded more, but it was that they *earned* the amount of points needed for that reward. If they chose to behave the whole week, do their chores the whole week, do their homework the whole week; therefore they got that many points. If they chose to goof off a couple of nights and maybe not do their chores, I did not have to get into a screaming match with them—they just didn't earn their points at the end of the day. This system is very, very effective!

You might want to give them something special every day. We try to stay away from candy (see Chapter 3 and What You Eat Matters). If you want to give them a treat, you can use a sticker, healthy fruit bar, etc. I don't know if I would encourage giving them a treat every day for behaving. We like to go with the point system or the sticker system because we don't want them to behave just because they are getting a treat. The difference between giving them points or stickers vs. a treat is that at the end of the night I can go to the chart and see if they have done their chores, done their homework, made right behavior choices and give them their sticker along with some free time. That is our choice because through experience it has worked for us. Others may do it differently. You know your kids better than anybody else, so experiment and see what works for you.

Last we want to talk about ways to alter behavior—the steps we take to alter behavior. Alter means to change, to cause to be different. Alteration is the act or process of making a change. So to alter behavior means that we need to help the child to understand that he or she needs to make a change. The first thing that you need to do is *establish the rules of your house.* Write them down and make them plain and clear (See Chapter 2, Getting Your House in Order). You can't expect the child to change their behavior if they don't know what they are doing wrong! If they don't know what is the right thing to do and the right way to act, they can't be expected to change (if they are doing something wrong and they don't even understand that).

In most classrooms in the schools, the first thing they do is to establish the rules. They hang them up on a board and they say, "This is what we expect of you," and then they have some kind of a system connected to the rules. Well, you need to do the same thing at home and follow that example at home.

Number 2 in the steps we take to alter behavior is to *establish the consequences for breaking one of the rules.* Write them down. They need to understand what happens if they break a rule. We have talked about rewards and consequences and they need to be followed through on every time! Remember that we talked about consistency, *consistency*, ***consistency***, especially with the strong-willed child. They will test you over and over and over again to see what they can get away with—to see how much "leeway" they have. They're thinking, "How far can I push it?" They will go right to the edge, before Mom's going to break, or before something is going to happen. They will push and push and push—push your button as far as they can.

Step Number 3 is *enforce the rules*. Follow through on your consequences and be consistent. Don't enforce the consequences one time, and then let it go another time. Your children will catch on and it will not be effective. Decide the consequence according to the outcome that you wish to achieve. Outgo = end result. What are you looking for? How do you want the child to respond? Let me give an example. Say that you are tired and have been at work all day long. This is so true—it has happened to me several times. You are at your wit's end, you are fed up, and are thinking that you would just like to go home and take a bubble bath, or lay in a Jacuzzi or read a book and put your feet up and relax. The last thing that you want to do is deal with your child's behavior if they have acted up in school again. Now if your child catches on to that, "Well, Mom's tired, so I'll just wait until she gets home and I know she wants to relax, and then I'm going to show her the note from school." And by that time you are very tired, and so you tell them, "Fine, fine, just go to bed." If you do not deal with it, your child will catch on and will repeat that scene every time. If you want them to alter their behavior and see them make right choices, then you need to teach them that immediately, *immediately* when something happens you will deal with them and have them suffer the consequences. You need to be consistent and follow through with the rules. You cannot wait or put it off until the next day, because usually by then you will have forgotten about it and the child has gotten away with it. And that is the absolute last thing that you want to happen.

Next we will talk about types of behavior that require an immediate consequence. Bad behavior is something that you choose to do. You consciously make a choice to misbehave or break a rule. This is different than a bad habit, which is something you do involuntarily, sometimes even without thinking because you have not been trained properly. Let's look at the difference. For example, when we got our four-year-old daughter she sucked her thumb, and sucked her thumb and sucked her thumb. It was cute at age four, but when you get to be 9 or 10 it's not cute anymore. However, it is not the same as bad behavior, it is called a bad habit. So there is a difference between negative behavior (making a conscious choice to do something wrong) and something that is done out of habit.

The following is a list of inappropriate behaviors:

1. *Disobedience*—total disrespect for authority. Totally not allowed. (See Chapter 2, Getting Your House in Order) Never allow your child to disrespect someone in authority—you as the parent or guardian, the teacher, a pastor or minister at church, a policeman, a counselor, a babysitter, or whoever is in authority! There must be an immediate consequence for that.

2. *Lying* is totally not allowed, no matter if they are in trouble or not. We tell our children that if they have done something wrong, there is a consequence. But if they lie and do not tell the truth then they will get a double consequence. You will be in trouble for what you have done and in trouble for lying, so you will pay a double consequence. Most of the time they learn very quickly to tell the truth, even though they know that they will still have a

consequence. Many people say, "Oh, that was so nice that you told the truth that we'll let it go this time." No! Wrong choice! Because then your child will always tell the truth, but continue to keep doing the bad behavior. They must still pay the consequence for making the wrong choice, and if they lie about it, they get double. And we always tell them that if they lie we will find out, whether we have to go and talk to a teacher or whatever, we always find out the truth and you can never get away with lying.

3. *Stealing* has an immediate consequence.

4. *Inappropriate Language.* Children should be taught that they are not allowed to cuss or swear at an adult or even at another child. That is inappropriate language.

5. *Temper Tantrums.* They are not going to get their own way. For example, in a store (I've seen this many times and it really irks me) the child will be on the floor screaming and throwing a temper tantrum and the parent is embarrassed and therefore gives in to the child and gets them what they want. Wrong choice! That teaches them that any time they want something, no matter where they are, they can throw a temper tantrum and embarrass their parent and get whatever they want. No! Do not let your child manipulate you. They should never be allowed to throw a temper tantrum.

6. *Rebellion*—total disregard for all rules. Absolutely not allowed! It needs an immediate consequence.

It is very strong, so consequences are doubled for rebellion.

Now we are doing some defining again so that we can understand exactly what disobedience is. Disobedience is refusal or failure to obey (meaning to comply with the command or order given); refusing to act quietly and quickly to the command given by the person in authority; disrespectful, lack of respect or esteem towards the person in command; lack of honor; lack of consideration; total disregard.

There are three types of consequences for disobedience.

1. Natural consequences.
2. Work consequences.
3. Sense consequences.

A natural consequence is something that would interrupt a normal routine. If they choose to be lazy and play instead of clean their room, often wrong choices bring with them their own set of consequences. For example, you could make them exercise, like doing push-ups during the time when they would normally sleep or play. That would be a natural consequence.

Work consequences would be related to them not doing their chores. As a consequence, they would not only have to do their chores, but also have a whole day of work with no playtime. That's a work consequence. They had extra work time besides their normal chores during a time when they would usually have playtime. They can't get away with not doing their chores, because they still have to do the chore and the next day will do double now—because they chose not to do it now they have to do double. Especially if it happens on a Saturday they would have to spend their whole free day doing work instead of play. Or on a Friday that is family fun night, they have to work instead of have the fun night. It teaches them very quickly and I guarantee you that the next week it will not happen. They don't like to do work! Another example of a wrong choice (if you have older children) is when you leave to go to the store and give them a chore to do while you are gone and you have told them "No videos or TV while I'm gone—you've got your chores to do." If they make a wrong choice and watch something—I can always tell by the channels that were watched last on the remote whether or not they have been watching cartoons while I was gone—they are going to pay a work consequence. You have to know your own children.

Senses consequences are consequences that affect one or more of the five senses: eyes, ears, mouth, nose, and touch. The example that I gave you earlier was of something that our son didn't like to eat (the sauerkraut). It was a very effective consequence for our son. We used this as an effective form of discipline for him because he absolutely hates sauerkraut.

Knowing your child's personality and what works for them is also very important. We've talked about active vs. passive personalities. We must change the pattern or response of a child with a negative behavior that is triggered by a situation. Remember that our ultimate goal is to alter or change the behavior pattern. And also remember that it takes at least 30 days to change a pattern or cycle.

I'm going to touch on something that may be controversial. A lot of people like to use "time out" as a form of discipline, but I personally am against it. Time out does not get to the root of the problem. It's like the band-aid example. A band-aid doesn't heal a cut, the cut needs to be taken care of in order to completely heal. The band-aid covers up the cut so that you don't see it any more. But when you take the band-aid off, the problem is still there. The behavior has not been altered when a child is put in time out. It may calm the child down temporarily, because they are sitting in the chair and calming down, but have you actually altered the behavior?

- The next time that situation occurs, is your child going to make a different choice?
- Or are they going to make the same choice again?

You need to choose something that will actually change the behavior. Here are some examples of things that have worked for us. For stealing you can take something away from them that they really like. Hold it in front of them and let them see it or hear it (it could be a DVD or something) and then break it and take it away. Let them know how it feels to have something of theirs taken that they loved. For destroying property, such as a chair, tell them that they will have to stand at the table during meals since they destroyed their chair. They have lost the privilege of having a chair to sit on during mealtime, because they destroyed the chair.

We hope that you understand the difference between discipline and punishment and that you have learned some things about what creative discipline is. You will get results if you make the consequence appropriate to the offense and if you are consistent!

We want to share some of our results with you in the next chapter.

Chapter 8

Applications and Results

This chapter deals with what will happen after you have done everything we have talked about in the previous seven chapters: *How to Get Started, Getting Your House in Order, What You Eat Matters, Knowing Your Body and How it Functions, Words are Powerful, Understanding Temperaments and Personality, and Creative Discipline.* I want to share with you what the applications and results are from our personal experience. This is not something that we just made up; we adopted four African-American children at the ages of 4, 5, 6, and 7 and they all had behavior issues, were on medication, and were doing poorly in school. We had been told that because of their issues, they would need to be medicated for behavior problems for the rest of their lives.

Our results did not happen overnight; it took time, consistency and doing everything that we have talked about in the first seven chapters. But through the process of being diligent, through not giving up, but by being consistent we have achieved the following results.

I am sharing this with you because I truly believe that every family that is really seeking an alternative to putting their children on medication for what are deemed as "behavior issues" would have the same results, if they would follow the exact same pattern.

When we first got the children, they all had behavior issues, were doing poorly in school, were labeled as mentally delayed, and were in counseling and on medication. The side effects of the behavior medication caused them to have loss of appetite and the inability to sleep. So they were taking medication for *those* problems. The sleeping medication caused them to sleep so soundly that they were unable to sense the need to go to the bathroom and they would end up wetting the bed every night.

So what I am talking about is a process that took place for us. Because of the restrictions we were under in the Children's Services system, we could not wean the children totally off medication for the first nine months that we had them. After we went to court and the adoption was finalized, we took the children off of medication totally with the exception of our second son. He was on such a high dosage of medication (60 mg of Ritalin/day, which was 15 mg. 4 times a day), that under the advice of the doctor that he was currently seeing, we gradually lowered the dosage. Because it was the middle of the school year, he suggested that we wait until summertime to totally take him off. When the children started back to school in September of that year, they were in Kindergarten, Pre-First, First, and Third. That was the year when they were totally off all medication. The results I am about to share are since they have all been medication free and they are still medication free and are continuing to excel to this day!

I will start first with my oldest son. For the past three years he has received the Principal's Award, which means that he has had all A's on his grade card, along with an Excellent behavior report. He received the

Helping Hand award for willingness to lend a hand to other students who needed help. In Fourth grade he was one of only two students in the school to pass all five parts of the Ohio Proficiency Test the very first time. He was chosen by the principal to attend the Jeremy Lincoln Foundation luncheon as one of the school's representatives, because of his academic record and excellent behavior. My son has also received Perfect Attendance Awards for the past three years. He has not missed even one day of school. He was chosen in Fourth Grade to be a Safety Patrol Guard, and this was unusual because normally only fifth and sixth graders were allowed to be guards. But because they did not have enough fifth and sixth graders with excellent behavior records they asked my son if he would like to be a guard. He, of course, was thrilled. In third grade he helped with the school fundraiser. The school was trying to raise enough money to buy a marquee sign for the school. They needed to raise over $10,000. He raised more money than anyone else in the third grade and won the top seller award.

He is also actively involved in our church, besides achieving academic awards and successes at school. At church he is a Jr. Usher and he is faithful and on time every week. At present he is in training to be a Teacher in the Children's Church and is also getting ready to go on a Mission trip to Guatemala where he and others will work in an orphanage for 500 children. He will be able to share from some of the experiences he has had with the children there. He has climbed to Level 7 in the Children's Church by memorizing Scriptures and memorizing the list of all of the books in the Bible.

This year in addition to all of this he is on his school's basketball team. He is the starting center for the team and in order to keep that position he must maintain his excellent behavior record and continue to excel in his grades. These are just some of the accomplishments that he has achieved since being off the medication. In addition, when he was in sixth grade he was nominated by one of his teachers to receive a scholarship to The Ohio State University and was accepted to receive a FULL scholarship as long as he maintains at least a 3.0 grade point average throughout Jr. High and High School, continues his excellent behavior record, and continues to have parental involvement. There's no problem there as my husband and I are both very involved in our children's lives. All of this happened in spite of the fact that we were told when we got him that he "was mentally under-developed and would never excel" and that he would have to be placed in one of the behavior problem classrooms.

And I mustn't forget about the essay contest he entered. He had to write an essay about "Why I love my Mom and Dad." The essay that he wrote was a State winner for his grade level. He was asked to read his essay at the School Board meeting in front of the Superintendent, Board members, and many school representatives. They were all very proud of him and this relates to each of my other children, as I will share later as I talk about their accomplishments. The School Board was very pleased because it was the first time that anybody from his school had ever won anything at the state level. At the time of the writing of this book, he is getting ready to attend Jr. High School. My husband and I are very proud of him and we know that he will continue to accomplish whatever he sets his mind to do.

At this point let me say that I realize that the results that we are seeing from the application of the principles in this book are not only remarkable, but also even incredible. If you are finding it hard to believe that what I am telling you is true, then there will be a list of witnesses in the next chapter who would be delighted to talk with you and confirm that what we are saying is absolutely true.

Our middle son, who was the biggest challenge for us and was on the very high dosage of Ritalin and had to be weaned off it over the period of a year, has been on the Honor Roll for the last three years. This means that he received all A's and B's on his grade card. He also has received Perfect Attendance awards for the last three years. In the First Grade he won the Dynamite Student award for being an excellent student. He was asked by the teacher to help with the Second Step program. This program is to help students deal with their feelings. We were told that he had a lot of compassion for others. He helped other children by reading to them and helping them with their schoolwork. He also helped with the School Fundraiser and won the top seller prize for his grade. He loves Art and is very good at it and he is currently involved with a Computer Graphic Art program and he hopes to excel with it. Actually he will succeed very well with it because he already is!

At church he is a Jr. Greeter. He is also chosen weekly to help teach children by being involved in skits and drama.

Our son when he was in Fourth Grade was continuing to excel. He passed the Fourth Grade Reading Proficiency Test in Third Grade, so he does not even have to take it again in the Fourth Grade. Last, but not least, he also won the State-wide essay contest for the First Grade level by writing his essay on, "Why I Love my Mom and Dad." We are very proud of him.

My oldest daughter has received the Principal's Award for two years by getting all A's on her grade card. She has also won the Wise Worker award in Second Grade by getting 100 percent on all of her Spelling tests.

And she won the High Flying Success award for 100% on Vocabulary in 1998 and the #1 Participation Award for 100% in Reading in 1999. She also made the Cheerleading team this year at school.

At church she is called the Good Samaritan helper, because she is one of the best helpers that they have. She is conscientious and always on time. She is presently a Jr. Greeter and is in training to run the Sound System in the Children's Church. She has achieved a high level in the Children's church by memorizing several Scriptures and learning the Books of the Bible. For the past two years she has been involved in the Dance ministry at church. She is on the Jr. Dance team and absolutely loves it. She won the same Statewide Essay contest at her grade level for her essay on "Why I Love my Mom and Dad."

Our youngest daughter is the one we got at the age of four. She started out in Pre-School and has currently been on the Honor Roll for the last three years, maintaining all A's and B's. In a couple of quarters she got straight A's. She won the Star Student award for the ABC chant in First Grade. She received a Safety City award for attending that program and passing all of the parts of it. She also has three years of Perfect Attendance awards. My daughter loves to sing and dance. She was chosen to be one of the Kay Cook dancers at school and she has performed dances all over that have helped her to learn about her African-American heritage. In her first year of taking professional dance, she performed in the production of *Broadway Kids* at the Stranahan Theatre in Toledo, Ohio. She also helped with the school fundraiser and was the # 1 seller for the entire Kindergarten class and won top prize. This past year she finally achieved her goal of making the Principal's list for the first time. She worked very hard to achieve this.

At church she is presently a Jr. Greeter, and she has achieved Level 3. She is also on the Dance team at church. Because she is very tall for her age and also a little bit younger than the other girls, she has had to work very hard to stay in this group, but she absolutely loves it. At church she is not only on the Dance team, but also on the Praise and Worship team for Children's church and she has been a helper in many areas at church.

And are you ready for me to mention that my baby, my youngest, also entered and won the Essay contest for her grade level with her essay on "Why I Love my Mom and Dad."? At this point I should tell you that the judges were different at each grade level and they did not know who had been chosen at the other grade levels. I was told that the judges broke down and cried when they read my children's essays. When one of the judges went into another judge's room and showed them my daughter's essay that had been chosen, the second judge said, "Well, I have one here that you just have to read!" It happened to be my son's. When I received the phone call to let me know that my children's essays had been chosen, the lady said that she had been very touched and could tell that the essays had been written from their hearts and that they were very sincere. All four of my children received a plaque and recognition at a special Forum. What made it touching for us was what the plaque actually read, "This award is for the parents of (child's name) for their outstanding job of rearing (child's name) with core values, faith, love, and the basic needs of life."

Besides all of this, my older son gave a speech when he received the award on how much that we meant to him—*on how much we meant to him!* Do I sound like a proud parent? Well, I am! To see how far that the children have come, and to know that this is only the beginning, brings tears to my eyes. I'm sure that there will be much more to tell as time goes on. But for now I'm just thankful for where we are, for where they have come from, and for the results that we have seen.

I share this with you because I believe that every family that is struggling with issues or behavior problems, etc. who truly care for and love their children and want to see them changed, can have the same results if they diligently follow what I have shared with you in the past seven chapters. I am writing this from my heart. I truly believe that it can happen and I can't wait to hear the results achieved in *your* family after you have put these principles into practice!

Results In My Family

CHAPTER 9

Summing Up

People often ask me:

- To what do you attribute the success of your children?

In giving this question serious thought, my answer would be, I believe two factors were necessary—

- *Our strong religious beliefs*
- *The amount of time we have spent with our children.*

Our children are not bounced back and forth from sitter, to their grandparents, or to a daycare until Mom finally picks them up. My children had that experience in the foster care system. I as their mother make sure that my whole day revolves around my children and their needs. For instance, if they need me to be in their classroom, I am there. If they need a driver or chaperone for their field trip, I make sure that I am available. When there is an assembly at school or whenever my children are participating in a program, I am there to watch and cheer them on.

My children also need us to spend time with them in the evening. They want and need Mom or Dad to help them with their homework, to read to them, to spend time listening to them talk about their day, or just to hold them on our laps and give them attention. An important family time is when we eat dinner together every night. This is a lost art—everyone sitting down together at the table to eat a home cooked meal. During this time, our children take turns sharing with us how their day went. Its is a peaceful, uninterrupted time that the whole family can share with one another.

Spending recreation time or just plain fun with our children is important also. We have family fun nights, where we may play *Monopoly*, *How to Become a Millionaire*, or some other fun, relaxing game. Besides this, going out sometimes is also important. Skating, or bowling, or going to a movie is important family time.

Last, but certainly not least, we pray with our children. Our children need Mom and Dad both to be willing to pray with them anytime that they need it.

So in summing up, investing time into your children does not go to waste! The return on your investment is enormous.

- *Is it a sacrifice?* **Yes!**
- *Is it easy to do?* **No!**

But in the long run, you reap what you sow.
Are we seeing results because of this? Absolutely!

Notes

Challenges:

Goals:

What can I begin to do right now?

CHAPTER 10

The Witnesses

Witness 1

I met the Anderson family at a special awards ceremony where a community group was giving awards to parents of children who had written the best essays about "Why I Love My Mom and Dad". I spoke to the Andersons and their children and learned of their amazing journey through adoption. I learned how they struggled to mold together as a family, while dealing with issues of race, prior neglect, and diagnoses of the children with Attention Deficit Disorder resulting in significant medication.

The Andersons' award recognized them for their outstanding job of rearing their children with core values, faith, love, and the basic needs of life. The Anderson children's essays about their parents were touching and inspiring. Their story is one that should be heard and learned from.

Peter R. Silverman
President of the School Board
Toledo Public Schools

Witness 2

Mr. and Mrs. Anderson have always kept communication open with their children's teachers and myself. Parents as partners in the educational process has been the number one reason their children have been and will continue to be successful in life. They attend to details and push positive values with their children.

Patricia Jimison
Principal
Toledo Public Schools

Witness 3

As the Assistant Principal of the Anderson's children's school, I have come to know the Anderson family. Mr. and Mrs. Anderson are a vital part of our team at the school. I would like to list just some of the activities they have either initiated or been a part of:

a. Parent Teacher Organization.
b. Donation of a copier.
c. The purchase of our new outdoor school sign.
d. Christmas program based on love presented to our K-2 children two years now and giving everyone a candy cane.
e. Making available various resources to the entire teaching staff of the school, including donating reams of copier paper to each teacher every month.
f. Monthly parenting sessions offered to the parent population of the school at no charge. With this they offered free childcare, food, handouts to each parent, and follow-up care with various resources and words of encouragement, and tons of love and compassion.

I am sure that there are many other things I have forgotten to include, such as both Anderson parents being involved in their children's classrooms almost on a daily basis. Driving for field trips and being present in the lunchroom has also contributed to their being such a constant fixture at the school, that it would be easier if I could outline when they are not there.

Using their family seminars they have touched so many lives and saved so many children because their parents have learned more appropriate responses to their children's behavior. I have learned a tremendous amount of skills that I incorporate into my own parenting techniques. It has been a breath of fresh air to work with people who are devoted to people. It has brightened the hallways of our school and has truly affected the behavior of the children. Keeping HIM in the focus of all the Andersons do has made our school a better place to be.

Michelle Tuite
Assistant Principal
(presently, Principal)
Toledo Public Schools

Witness 4

I met Linda in 1999 while I was serving as acting Assistant Principal of their school. She told me about their family. Like many other parents she raved about her children. It was wonderful to have a parent actively involved in their children's education. She relayed to me her family's story of strife and struggle. The Andersons had adopted four African-American children with a horrific story. The kids had attendance problems, academic deficiencies, and behavior issues. This is the typical description of inner-city African-American foster children that usually fall by the nature of the education system and then drop out of school. But for Russ and

Linda this was not an option. With a strong Christian foundation their story of revival began. Through tears, shouts, laughter, and pain, the Anderson children were destined for greatness. By changing the horrors and negative routines the children had embedded, all four children have realized success. Love, structure and discipline were key factors in their success.

It was this common thread that bonded me to the Andersons. I could truly see that Linda had a passion about not only educating her children, but others as well! As an educator I have often struggled with why students fall. Some educators believe it is culturally based, others feel it is social-economic factors, and still others feel that it is parental involvement. Although all three have merit and justification, I believe that parental involvement is the greatest contributing factor. Linda feels the same way. That is why she is so committed to being an active part of her children's education.

For Linda and Russ it has been a trying experience, but the rewards are almost unbelievable. Their story is true and noteworthy. The lessons contained in this book are life's lessons about child rearing. Remember everyone saying that there are no books or rules about raising children? I feel that the Anderson story can become a strong foundation to many struggling families that want what all parents want for their children—The Best!

Scott TenEyck
Principal and Friend
Toledo Public Schools

Witness 5

I was glad to see that Mrs. Anderson was writing a book, because I could speak volumes on behalf of the Andersons.

In one word, success!

I have known Russ and Linda Anderson and their children for almost five years. I have had the fortune of having three out of their four children in my third grade classroom. As a teacher I have been blessed with having Mrs. Anderson as a parent volunteer. She has been an integral part of my classroom, positively affecting my students and me! Her positive and motivated attitude is infectious.

Good things happen when Mr. and Mrs. Anderson are around.

I have seen so many improvements from the Anderson children, academically and socially, as a direct result from Mr. and Mrs. Anderson as parents. They have opened their home to four adopted children and shaped their lives with love. They have also paved a road for success for their children's lives. Faced with academically failing children, who faced many Challenges and had severe behavior problems, they were successful in nurturing four great kids!

Finally, Mr. and Mrs. Anderson are wonderful friends. Despite the fact that we have a professional relationship through school, I also consider the Andersons friends. They are more than willing to help in any capacity. We work well together and they have encouraged me to do my personal best. I am proud to call the Andersons my friends!

Jeffery D. Miller
3rd Grade Teacher
Toledo Public Schools

Witness 6

Being the Art teacher here at the Anderson children's school, I have noticed how well behaved the children are. The children seem to be very happy and showing a strong interest in their schoolwork. Also, I have noticed the children have adjusted well being African-American in an European American atmosphere home setting. Mr. and Mrs. Anderson are actively involved in their children's education and upbringing. Both parents spend a great deal of time with their children and it shows. It has been a great pleasure having the Anderson children in my classroom. Mrs. Anderson is a super volunteer, and she takes an active part in all that the children do. I know these children will grow up to be successful!

Ms. McCaster
Art Teacher
Toledo Public Schools

Witness 7

As a teacher, I have known Mrs. Anderson and her family for the past three years now. Mrs. Anderson is a very actively involved parent in the school. She sits on the board of the Parent/Teacher Organization (PTO), drives and chaperones for field trips, helps out in all her children's classrooms, and assists in any way she can for the betterment of the school. I recently got to know her older son better, as basketball coach of the school league. Her son is one of our star players. He not only plays an excellent center position, but has one of the best attitudes of any of the players. It is obvious he was taught some Christian values and respect of authority. Even if he does not like doing something he is told, he will obey anyhow and try it. It has been a pleasure to know the Anderson family. Their story is truly remarkable!

Fred W. Borden
Teacher, Basketball Coach
Toledo Public Schools

Witness 8

So you want to know about the Anderson family? How do they achieve the results they achieve, and how have so many positive changes been made in the lives of their four children? It has certainly been an exciting thing to observe the real and tangible effects of using the important principles of child training that Russ and Linda have used to shape and mold their four children.

I have known the Andersons for about nine years, and on a much more personal basis for about seven years. I remember when Russ and Linda decided to pursue adoption. I was somewhat apprehensive about the magnitude of their endeavor to adopt four children of African-American descent, since they are a Caucasian couple. In addition to the obvious cultural and racial issues that we face in today's society, many other factors played a role in my initial apprehension. The Andersons also did not have any children previous to the adoption. All of the children were of pre-school or elementary age, not babies that come with a much less probability of undesirable behavior or habits established. The children came from a home that had little or no structure. Also, they were previously diagnosed with learning and behavioral disabilities, complete with prescribed medication. I am thrilled to say that they proved my apprehensions to be unfounded!

The very direct involvement of Russ and Linda in their children's lives have brought about a truly dramatic change in all areas of the children's lives. The children all do very well academically, ranking at the top of their classes. The children are all heavily involved in the Children's Ministry at their church, participating in such things as dance, drama, greeters, ushers, and helping in sound. They are well-behaved and happy children! It is a pleasure to have them in our classes at church.

The Andersons have been very involved in helping children for many years. I was excited when Linda started a community program known as Family Enrichment Coalition (FEC). FEC is an exciting program founded by someone that can truly help other families that are struggling with the issues we face every day in life. I personally can attest that the principles and the information taught in the program comes from someone that can say, "been there, done that, made it work".

I was thrilled to hear of Linda's desire to write a book about the training, trials, and tribulations they have faced as parents. I believe that any information that Russ and Linda are willing to write down, and put in book form will be an invaluable tool, to see real and positive changes come to those that read and heed the life changing information.

Richard D. Maus
Minister of Children's Services
Cornerstone Church
Toledo, Ohio

Witness 9

The children placed with families who have strong religious beliefs, regardless of their faith, tend to excel! The Anderson children are a perfect example of this. They are one of our success stories!

Brit Eaton
Former Executive Director
Adopt-America
Toledo, Ohio

Witness 10

Ever since I met the Anderson family, I can't stop thinking about them and their remarkable story. I tell everyone I meet about them. The Anderson children are such a pleasure to talk with. They are so well-behaved and polite. The first time I met the family was at a forum where they were about to receive an award for winning a contest. We bonded immediately and I have been in contact with them ever since. It is a pleasure for me to know this family!

Judge Andy Devine
Juvenile Court (Retired)
Toledo, Ohio

Witness 11

The Anderson family's success story is one that can be duplicated in thousands of homes, wherever there are parents who are willing to invest their time and attention towards the process of helping their children to achieve positive behavior. I strongly recommend this book as a practical handbook for reaching that goal.

Janet DeVriendt
Friend
Primary Reading Teacher,
Otsego Schools

My Witnesses

Bibliography

Ray Sahelian M.D., *Nature's Serotonin Solution,* Avery Publishing Group, Garden City Park NY 1998.

Elizabeth Somer, *Food and Mood,* Henry Holt Reference Books, New York NY 1995.

Robert Ullman, M.D. & Judyth Reichenberg-Ullman, M.D., *Ritalin Free Kids,* Prima Publishing, Roseville CA 2000.

About the Author

Linda J. Anderson is a wife and mother of four adopted children. Linda and her husband of twenty years have taught and trained children in many different areas. They have a heart and passion for underprivileged and inner city children. Although never having any children of their own, they felt a need to bring children into their home to train and raise to be a part of a family. Thus in 1995 they adopted four African-American siblings, two boys and two girls. Linda is the founder of Family Enrichment Coalition (FEC), an organization whose mission is to offer an alternative for families whose children have been diagnosed as having poor behavior patterns requiring the use of medication. Through FEC Linda teaches seminars and helps to train families in ways to enrich their lives. She was recently elected to the Lucas County Family Council as the Parent Representative. In addition, she and her husband Russell work with Adopt America adoption agency and are in training to become Adoption Specialists. This book was written as a tool and testimony from her own experience in order to help other families.

The Anderson Family in 1995

Author Contact Information

Linda J. Anderson

P.O. Box 13335

Toledo, OH 43613

E:mail: addornottobe@yahoo.com